HOW TO PAINT & DRAW
ANIMALS

**Written and Illustrated
by David Astin**

CRESCENT BOOKS
New York

Acknowledgments

The Publishers would like to thank the following for permission to reproduce their photographs: David Astin 18, 22, 26, 28, 34, 52, 54, 56, 58; Barnaby's Picture Library 60; Michael Holford 64 (top); Peter Newark's Western Americana 64 (bottom); The Tate Gallery, London 64 (center).

Additional artwork by Liz Chapman.

Designed and produced by Intercontinental Book Productions Limited, Berkshire House, Queen Street, Maidenhead, Berkshire SL6 1NF.

Contents

Introduction

Although there is no doubt that drawing and painting animals is a very rewarding pastime, it is often difficult and frustrating because they have a tendency to move, walk, or fly away at the least opportune moment. To really learn to draw and paint them well, you must nevertheless persevere and work from life as much as possible. You may sometimes, like most animal artists, use photographic reference but, to learn about animal anatomy and structure, there is no substitute for being face to face with the real thing. It is only then that you really start to understand your subject intimately.

This book is not intended as a substitute for the experience of painting and drawing; it will provide a starting point and guide to such problems as construction and the use of different media and methods. Try to work through the book practicing as you go. The more difficult aspects of color and composition appear at the end of the book so that, when you have to deal with them, you will already have gained confidence and a method of working which suits you. Do not be discouraged if you cannot remember all the information about anatomy; it is intended primarily for reference. The most important point in all forms of artistic activity is actually doing it.

Approaches to drawing

There is a common misconception that there is a correct way to draw and paint, and that this can therefore be taught magically and with little effort on the part of the student. There are many ways to draw and all of them are equally valid. The cave painting produced by an unknown prehistoric artist which is presented at the end of the book has its own charm, and is as informative as the most photographically realistic work. The validity and importance of both styles of work arise from the personal involvement of the artist in his attempt to portray the world.

Painting and drawing is a subjective activity and can therefore only be taught in the light of personal experience. As you proceed and gain confidence you will automatically begin to reject and replace the information given with your own methods of working. This is both good and natural, and indicates progress. For the time being, however, it is important to realize that the comments contained in this book are one man's personal approach, presented to help you through the early days of great enthusiasm and little experience.

The drawings here indicate the variety of different ways one artist can tackle a subject. The owl was drawn with a mapping pen and Indian ink; the cat was drawn with charcoal; the dog

was drawn with an ink wash; the cheetah with pen and ink and the orang-utan with pencil. The choice of media will have a great influence on the appearance of the finished result. Even so, with experience, the artist can make different kinds of marks using the natural characteristics of the media. It is important for the beginner to get used to handling the different materials. By all means try as many as you wish — it will expand your options.

The cat illustrated was likely to change position at any moment, and the method of working suggests this. The basic form was scribbled in very swiftly, using charcoal, which has the ability to cover large areas quickly. Time, or the lack of it, has caused the restless nature of the subject to be captured. The limitation of time also makes mistakes in proportion inevitable. The correction of these mistakes by drawing over the top gives the drawing a feeling of life, so do not be afraid to make mistakes and correct them or leave them as you wish.

There are many instances of very fine work in which the proportion is not technically correct but which adds to the quality and charm of the completed piece. There are certain techniques which will be found useful, and these are presented in the following chapters.

There is one firm piece of advice worth remembering, and that is that the essence or character of the subject should be projected through your drawing, and should be allowed to influence the way you draw.

Materials

Anything that makes a mark, even a stick or a sponge, can be used as a drawing tool, and all tools and media have their own particular limitations and character which will influence the work. The materials below are only a selection from the vast range available; experience as many different media as possible and do not be afraid to experiment. The experience you acquire in this way will be invaluable.

Pencils

Pencils are the basic drawing implement. There are various grades suitable for line and tone work; try as many as you can and finally choose the ones you find most suitable. Colored pencils are suitable for small sensitive color studies.

Charcoal

Charcoal makes bold, impressive marks and sensitive, soft lines. It erases well and creates beautiful grays when smudged.

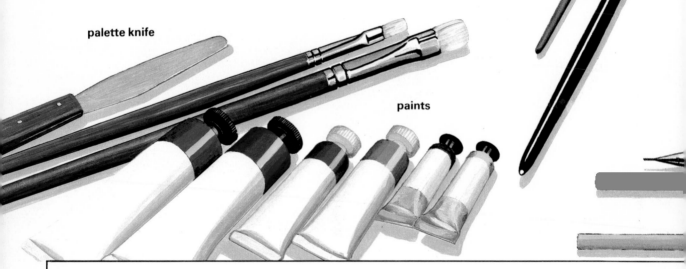

palette knife

paints

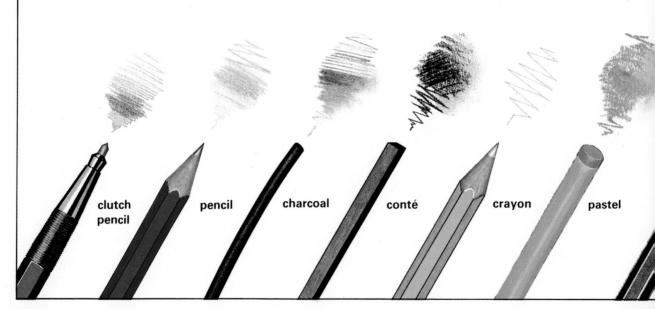

clutch pencil

pencil

charcoal

conté

crayon

pastel

Also, try conté, which is available in black, white and sepia. Pastel is also available in a variety of colors. It is soft and crumbly, and very effective on tinted paper; it should be used boldly and broadly.

Pen and ink

Pen and ink is another traditional medium well worth trying. Practice with every variety of pen you can find, from a dipper pen to a felt-tipped pen, since each type has a different quality.

paper

inks

Paints

Watercolor paint is available in pans and tubes. Buy the best quality; they are easier to use and make brighter and cleaner colors. Good sable brushes are the best to use and will last a lifetime if you take care of them. Hog hair brushes are useful for textured washes.

Oil color is available in tubes and cans. Buy the largest amounts that you can afford of a limited range of colors. You will need more white than any other color and smaller amounts of strong, dark colors. Hog hair brushes are the most suitable for this medium, but obtain a couple of soft brushes for glazing. It is necessary to have a variety of sizes of brush. If in doubt, buy brushes larger than you think you will need, since oil paint is a broad medium.

Although there are various surfaces traditionally accepted for each medium, try any and every surface you can find.

pentel　　dipper　　sable　　hog hair
　　　　　　pen　　　brush　　brush

9

Body shape and proportion

Each animal's characteristic shape has evolved according to its environment and way of life. In the case of domesticated animals, man has influenced the anatomical development by selective breeding for his own purposes. The relative proportion of the limbs of each animal can be seen by observing the amount of space occupied by the body shape within the square. In each of the illustrations, the left-hand side of the square has been drawn through the point of the shoulder, while the right-hand side has been dropped through the rear end of the pelvis.

It is important to grasp the overall body shape of your subject and the proportion of the limbs, head and neck to the main mass of the body.

Gauging and laying down these main proportions is the most difficult problem facing the beginner. It requires constant comparison of masses and angles while the drawing is in progress. The most common mistake is to become involved with the detail of the subject too soon while forgetting the overall view. The result can be a beautifully drawn head complete to the last detail on a body which is physically unable to support it. Consider the "negative" shapes of the form, such as the space between the legs with reference to the belly and the ground, and the points of the animal which line up, for example, the shoulder, the knee and the ankle.

All these clues will help you to construct your drawing accurately. Don't become discouraged, and do be prepared to make mistakes; error is your real teacher. Spend time thinking and looking at your subject and your drawing – it will be time well spent.

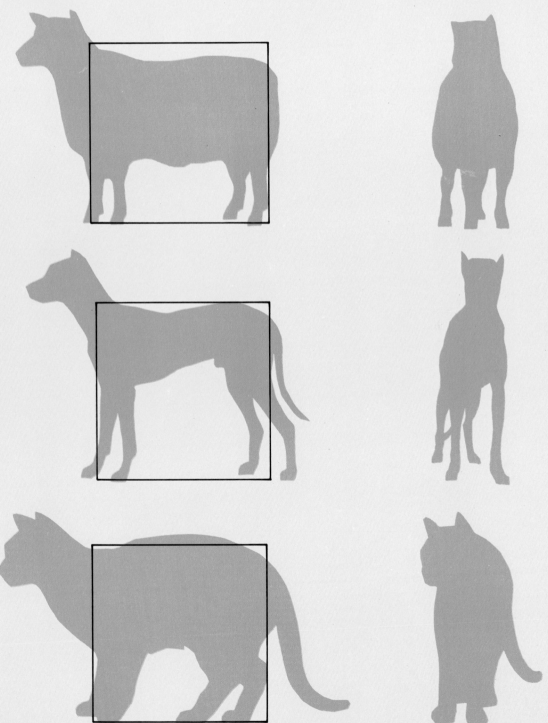

Techniques

Fur has been chosen as the subject to provide a few pointers concerning the way it can be rendered in various materials.

Pencil

Both the form and the texture of fur can be achieved by drawing selected sections of the hair, particularly at those points where the form changes direction, and the areas which are in shadow. Areas can be gradually darkened by hatching at different angles.

Colored pencil

Again, form and texture can be created by attention to the same points considered above. The richness and variety of color has to be built up by "overhatching" at different angles. This can be done with the point of the pencil leaving a space between the marks to show a certain amount of white paper, or with the side to create a continuous tone of color. This is known as glazing. The skill of colored pencil work is the ability to select and overlay different colors without creating a confused and muddy result.

Charcoal

This should be laid down with a bold "scribble" motion and then blended to a soft gray with the finger. Areas can be darkened by repeating the process, and highlights can be taken out using a kneaded eraser which has been moulded to a point. The material is ideal for recreating the soft fur of long-haired animals such as Persian cats.

Pastel

Very similar to charcoal in application, colors must be built up by hatching as with colored pencils. A roll of paper can be used to blend the colors together. This is a broad medium, and care is required to prevent smudging and muddy colors. A neutral-tinted paper (gray or fawn) is ideal to show off the light pastel shades to the best advantage.

Pen and ink

The direction of the hair can be indicated by line work. Try breaking up the line into dashes and dots on the light areas of form or, if using a line board, or very heavy paper, by scraping with a scalpel. Darker areas should be overlaid with cross-hatched lines. A scribble motion can be used if the nibs you are using will stand up to the violent changes of direction.

Brush and ink

Drawing in ink can be very direct as shown here or you can dilute the ink with water and work in washes. Use a large brush to lay down the initial wash following the changing directions of the form. When the first wash has dried, selected areas may be darkened with layers of wash, either of the same color or a different color. Each wash should be allowed to dry unless a blended effect is required. This, however, can be difficult to control. Finally, suggest the direction of the hair using a small brush.

Introduction to anatomy

You are not expected to memorize the position and name of every bone in an animal's skeleton. However, if you take animal drawing seriously, you should understand what underlies the exterior form and which positions or movements are physically possible. The most important features of the skeleton are common to many vertebrates, including man, and they share the same names. In fact, you can learn a lot about the animal skeleton by comparing it to your own.

The most obvious difference between the four-legged animal and man is the design of the leg and foot bones. Most animals walk on their toes with their "heel" and "wrist" held high off the ground. The horse, for example, walks on only one toe, the others having atrophied.

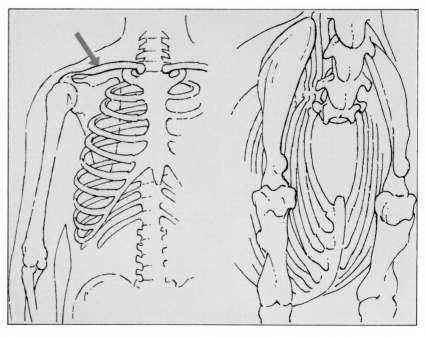

Another important difference is the lack of a developed collar bone (arrowed) – although it is present in some climbing animals like the squirrel. The horse's foreleg is attached to its body only by a muscle, but this is able to absorb a great deal of concussion that would otherwise be transmitted to the spine.

Nearly all animals, including man, have seven vertebrae in the neck. The size and flexibility varies according to the animal's feeding habits. Similarly, the number of dorsal and lumbar

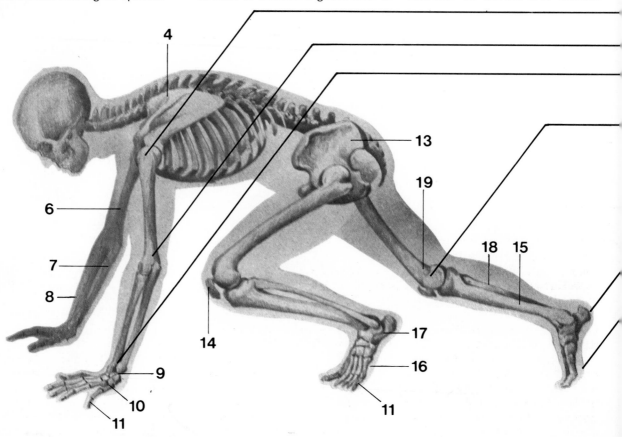

Key:
1. Skull
2. Mandible
3. Cervical vertebrae
4. Scapula
5. Sternum
6. Humerus
7. Ulna
8. Radius
9. Carpus
10. Metacarpus
11. Phalanges
12. Rib cage
13. Pelvis
14. Patella
15. Tibia
16. Metatarsus
17. Tarsus
18. Fibula
19. Femur
20. Coccygeal vertebrae
21. Point of the ischium
22. Sacral vertebrae
23. Lumbar vertebrae
24. Dorsal or thoracic vertebrae
25. Atlas or first cervical vertebrae

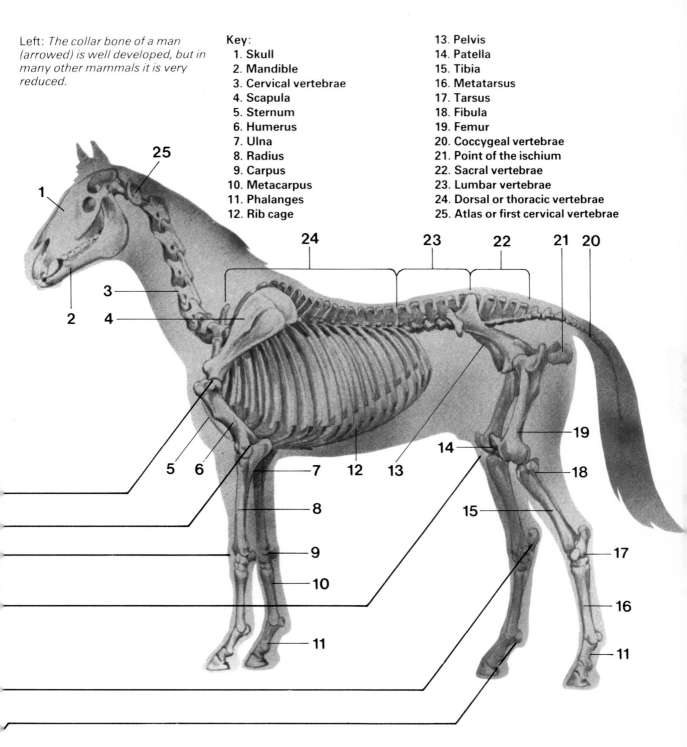

Left and above: *Comparison of the skeletal structure of a man with that of a horse.*

vertebrae in the spine are about the same but they, too, vary in size and shape, giving the characteristic back contour of each species. Lateral movement in the lumbar vertebrae (our waist) is very much restricted in a horse, but a carnivore like the cat can twist its body easily. The position and shape of the pelvis also varies a great deal (compare the pelvis of a man to that of a horse). Similarly, the skull is noticeably different and has developed according to the animal's feeding habits (compare a cat's skull to the horse's skull). Notice also, particularly in the case of a man, the relative area occupied by the brain.

In the following chapters about the basic structures of the dog, cat and horse you will be introduced to the main points of the structure of each animal's skeleton. The same applies to the chapters dealing with form. These chapters are intended to help you to construct your drawings by providing information which is not immediately visible in your subject.

Dogs: basic structure

Dogs, particularly large short-haired varieties like the labrador, are ideal subjects for studying animal anatomy. As you are drawing, imagine the skeleton underlying the hair and muscle and try to identify some of the main bones and joints.

There is little doubt that the domestic dog is related to the wolf and jackal. The skeleton of a large dog is so similar to that of a wolf that it is difficult to tell them apart. The spine of a dog consists of seven vertebrae in the neck (cervical), thirteen in the back (dorsal or thoracic), seven in the loins (lumbar), three sacral and twenty to twenty-two in the tail (coccygeal). In both the

dog and the wolf there are thirteen pairs of ribs, and both animals have forty-two teeth. They also both have five front and four hind toes.

The shape and position of all these bones are illustrated by the skeleton below. However, take note of several "landmarks" which will be important in the drawing's construction.

If you can remember to look for these points you will be able to construct a very simple structure based on the skeleton. The drawings below show how this structure of lines works in a variety of positions. Look for the direction of the spine and the angle of the shoulders and haunches (pelvis). If these angles and proportions are judged badly, your drawing will be built upon an inaccurate foundation. It is vital to get that basic construction correct, so practice drawing just the lines

formed by the main bones of your subject and you will soon learn to "feel" when a drawing is correct.

Key:
 1. **The angle of the scapula (shoulder blade).**
 2. **The protruding top end of the humerus (point of the shoulder).**
 3. **The protruding top end of the ulna (point of the elbow).**
 4. **The change in direction of the leg at the carpus (foreknee) which corresponds to the wrist in humans.**
 5. **The joint of the metacarpus and the phalanges on the front and hind legs (ball of foot).**
 6. **The back end of the tarsus (heel).**
 7. **The joint of the femur and tibia.**
 8. **The point of the ischium (rounded back end of the pelvis).**
 9. **The joint of the femur with the pelvis.**
10. **The crest of the ilium (the front end of the pelvis).**
11. **The protruding wing of the atlas or first cervical vertebrae.**
12. **The back of the skull.**

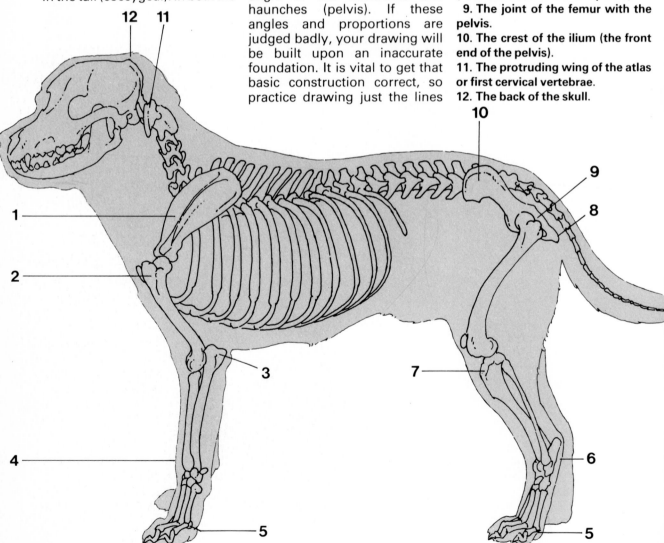

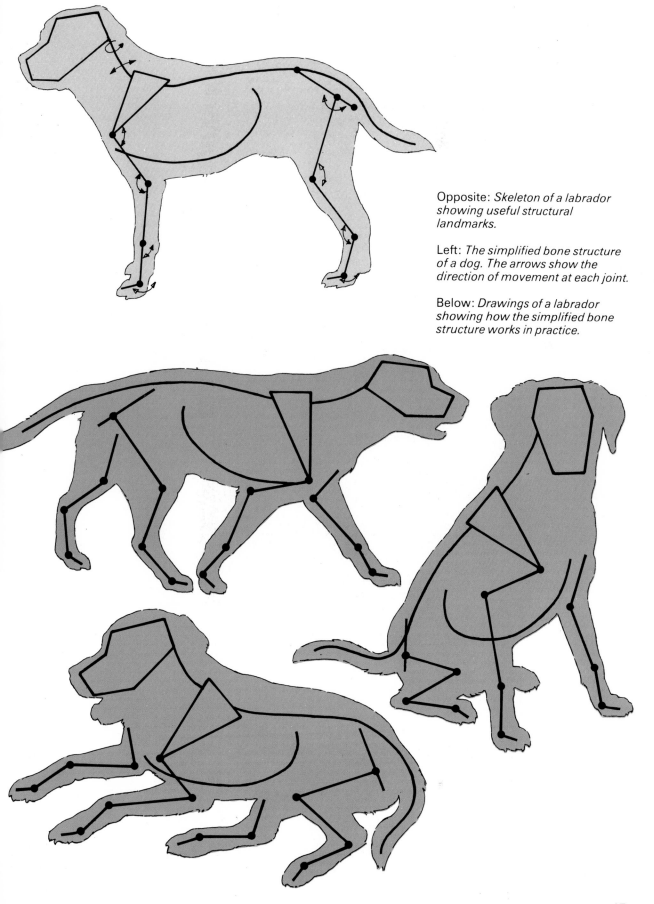

Opposite: *Skeleton of a labrador showing useful structural landmarks.*

Left: *The simplified bone structure of a dog. The arrows show the direction of movement at each joint.*

Below: *Drawings of a labrador showing how the simplified bone structure works in practice.*

Dogs: basic form

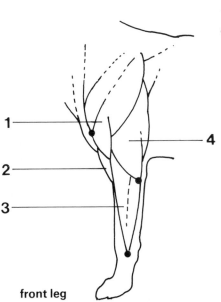

front leg

1
2
3
4

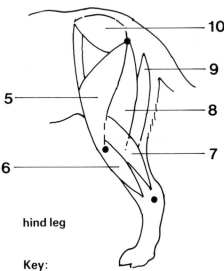

hind leg

5
6
10
9
8
7

Key:

1. **The deltoid muscles across the scapula.**

2. **The biceps at the front of the humerus.**

3. **The extensor and flexor metacarpi at the front and back of the lower leg.**

4. **The triceps, back of humerus.**

5. **The triceps over the femur.**

6. **The flexor metatarsi at the front of the tibia.**

7. **The gastrocnemius (calf muscle).**

8. **The biceps, back of femur.**

9. **The semitendinosus behind the biceps.**

10. **The gluteus medius from the front to the back of the pelvis.**

The muscles and ligaments which control the movement of the bones produce a complex network of layers which create the form of the body. The shoulder, buttock (haunch) and leg muscles are particularly developed and I have drawn diagrams of these two areas to help you establish the main muscles. You should be able to identify them on the photograph. On the forelegs and hindlegs the muscles that are apparent on the surface are listed in the key.

In order to understand the formation of the muscles it is a good idea to visualize the body as simple, geometric volumes. As the drawing progresses sections can be added and cut away until a more natural form emerges. Try to visualize the surface as a pattern of planes or facets and you will find it easier to compare angles and shapes on the drawing with those of the subject. Use a pencil held at arm's length to compare lengths or angles.

We do not know when the dog first became domesticated, but man has certainly influenced the evolution of the large variety of breeds we find today. Some

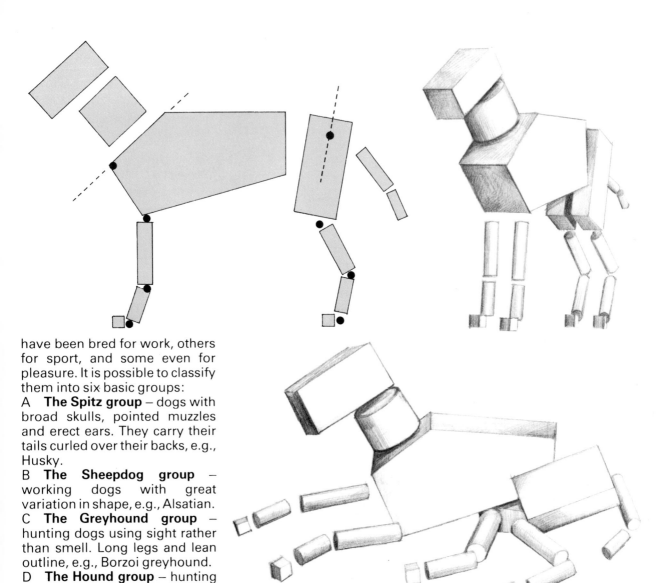

have been bred for work, others for sport, and some even for pleasure. It is possible to classify them into six basic groups:

A **The Spitz group** – dogs with broad skulls, pointed muzzles and erect ears. They carry their tails curled over their backs, e.g., Husky.

B **The Sheepdog group** – working dogs with great variation in shape, e.g., Alsatian.

C **The Greyhound group** – hunting dogs using sight rather than smell. Long legs and lean outline, e.g., Borzoi greyhound.

D **The Hound group** – hunting dogs using smell rather than sight. Long pendant ears, chunky faces, e.g., Basset hound.

E **The Mastiff group** – large bulky dogs, flat muzzles, e.g., Boxer.

F **The Terrier group** – wiry-coated, small to medium size, but strong and hardy, e.g., Airedale.

Above: *The form of a dog simplified into basic geometric volumes. The dotted lines indicate the angle of the shoulder and haunches, while the dots show the main joints.*

Left: *Examples of breeds from each of the six basic groups of dogs.*

Dogs: detail

Obviously, the hair and the details of the soft parts like the nose, ears and eyes, will vary not only from breed to breed but from individual to individual.

The direction of the hair, and the places where it divides or converges, are features worth noting. It is more ordered and complex than is often realized. Look at the front and hind quarters of a short-haired dog like a labrador. In fact, the correct drawing of hair direction can help to indicate form in your drawing. Do not overwork the detail of the hair so the form of the animal is lost. Not every hair needs to be carefully drawn in; suggestion is much better.

Detailed studies of noses, eyes, mouths and paws will be a great help when later drawing from the subject at a distance. They have certain structural characteristics which are common to all dogs, although details and proportions may vary. This is particularly the case with a dog's ears. Basically the ear is a

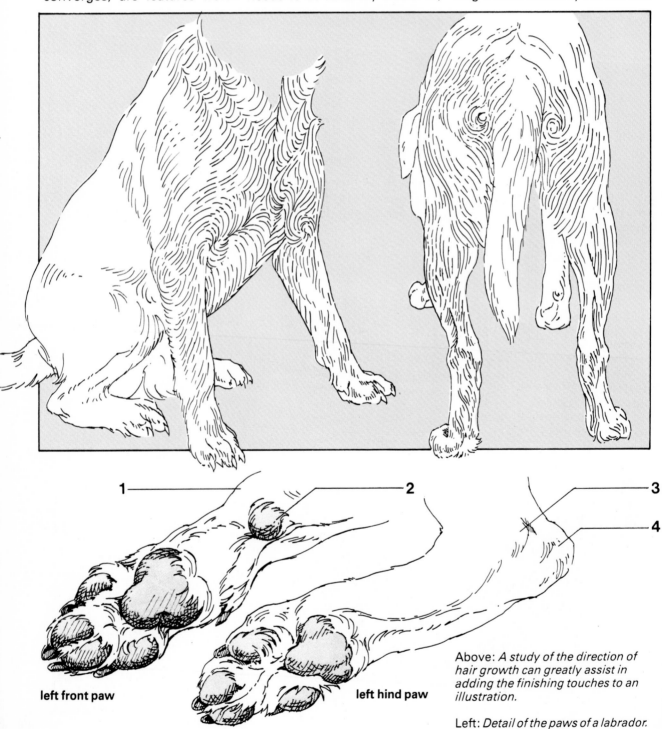

1 ——————————— 2 ——————————— 3

4

left front paw

left hind paw

Above: *A study of the direction of hair growth can greatly assist in adding the finishing touches to an illustration.*

Left: *Detail of the paws of a labrador.*

triangular sheet of cartilage rolled upon itself to form a funnel. In dogs that are always looking about them the ear muscles become highly developed and pricked ears have evolved, but the drooping ear (as in hounds) may be accounted for by underdeveloped muscles.

Key:
1. Carpus
2. Prisiform pad
3. Lower end of fibula
4. Tarsus
5. Fold of ear
6. Eye lid
7. Iris
8. Pupil
9. Nictitating membrane
10. Tear duct
11. Molars
12. Canines
13. Incisors

Below: *Understanding the structure of parts of the body greatly assists when adding detail.*

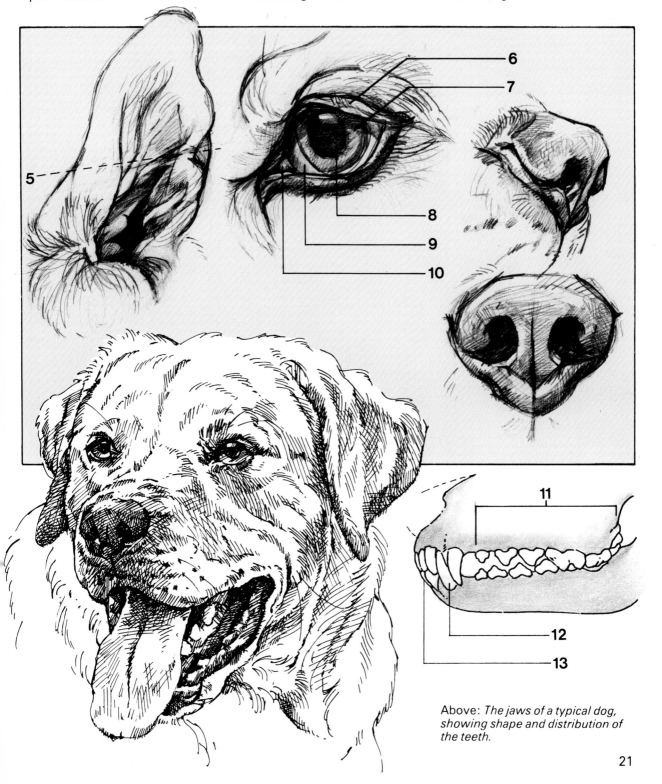

Above: *The jaws of a typical dog, showing shape and distribution of the teeth.*

Dogs: tackling a subject

Above: *An interesting study of a
labrador in pen and ink on line
board. A scalpel has been used to
break up the solidity of the line on
the shoulder and paws.*

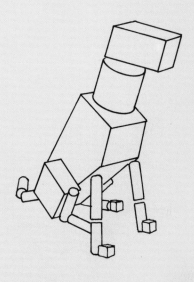

*Make sure that both you and your
subject are comfortable, you may be
willing to suffer for your art, but the
dog will not!*

*The first stage is to create a
simplified skeleton on the paper, to
correspond with that of the animal.*

*The volumes are now blocked in.
The proportions should be correct at
all stages of the procedure.*

Left: *Another view, this time in pencil. The alertness of the dog suggests that he is likely to move. You must be ready to accept unfinished drawings.*

Notice how the direction of the hair has been used to emphasize the form.

In the pencil drawing the form is created by a soft range of grays achieved by delicate shading which follows the direction of the hair or form, whichever appears to be applicable at the time.

The series of drawings on this page shows the advice given in previous chapters put into practice. Mark out a simple bone structure, paying particular attention to the position of the joints. Using the joints as a guide, draw upon the structure the basic form in simple volumes. Add to and cut away the structure to create a more naturalistic form, taking note of the muscles. Shade in pencil, emphasizing the volume by capturing the play of light across the form. Finally, draw in surface details such as hair direction and individual features such as ears, eyes, nose and feet.

These drawings show two different approaches to the same subject: one is drawn in line using ink, and the other is a tonal drawing in pencil.

Drawing directly in ink takes confidence and some practice, as any mark you make is permanent. Mistakes have to be drawn over and incorporated into the drawing, and this makes for a lively result. You can, of course, draw out the construction in pencil, then overdraw in ink, but I think this denies the expressive quality of line unique to a nib. An ink drawing has tremendous strength because of the contrast between the black marks and the white paper. Tone can only be created by building up a texture of lines or dots.

Modify the drawing making the image more life-like by cutting away and adding as necessary.

The basic detail is indicated. If the original drawing is kept light, it will not need erasing.

Tone is added to create a solid and rounded form. This will also help to cover the construction.

Cats: basic structure

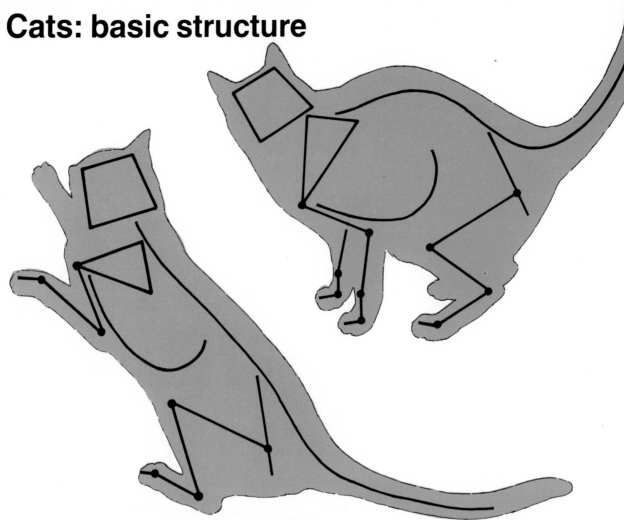

The cat's delicate and subtle proportions demand careful observation and sensitive drawing. The bones are rarely seen at the surface and, in contrast to the angular planes of the dog, a cat typically has a very round and soft, furry form. Very often, the subtle play of light on the fur, or the distortion of its markings, provide the only evidence of the underlying structure.

The cat has a lighter skeleton which is extremely flexible. It can curl up into a tight ball or suddenly appear twice its normal length when making a leap. The cat's legs, particularly its hind ones, are long relative to its body size, and although the cat is therefore extremely fast, it is not designed for prolonged activity. The chest cavity is small and narrow and consequently the heart and lungs are better suited for quick bursts of speed.

Above and opposite above: *Drawings of a cat showing how the simplified bone structure works in practice. Note the degree of flexibility of the spine.*

Below: *Skeleton of a cat showing useful structural landmarks.*

Opposite below: *The simplified bone structure of a cat. The arrows show the direction of movement at each joint.*

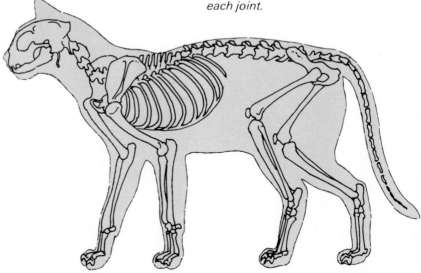

I have drawn a simplified bone structure of the cat. It is very similar to that of the dog. In fact, cats and dogs have the same number of vertebrae. The cat has a slimmer build, being narrower across the shoulders, the pelvis and the chest. The poses above will demonstrate the flexibility of the spine which the dog does not have to the same degree.

The direction and twist of the spine is probably the most important point to establish, followed by the angle of the shoulder blade and the pelvis. The gap between the shoulder blades, which rises above the spine, is particularly noticeable from a back view. The skull is very compact, giving the head a rounded appearance, and the neck is relatively short.

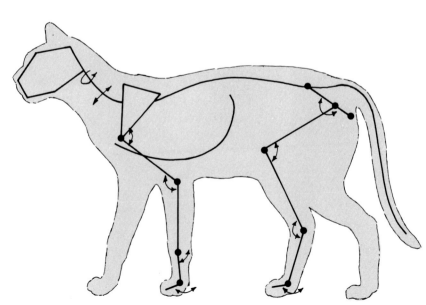

Cats: basic form and movement

Cats are carnivores; their muscles are adapted for freedom of movement. The muscles are especially developed in the back legs – giving a powerful spring – and across the neck and shoulders for striking and carrying prey.

As on pages 22 and 23, these drawings show the simple formula for drawing the form of the animal, and how the rigid volumes can be cut away and shaped to produce a more realistic form.

The sequence of movement shown below is based upon the action photographs of Eadweard Muybridge, and demonstrates how the walk (A-C) is accelerated through the lope (D-F) into a run (J-L).

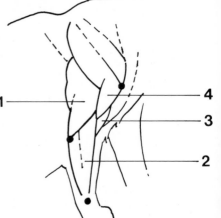

front leg

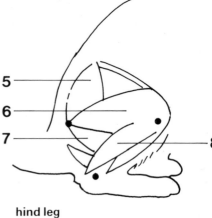

hind leg

Above: *Detail of the leg muscles.*

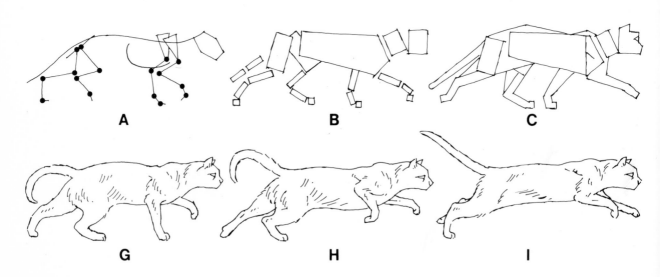

A

B

C

G

H

I

Above: *A. The basic skeleton is drawn in a simplified form.*

B. When the proportions appear correct, build up the volumes of the form.

C. Add further information to clarify the form.

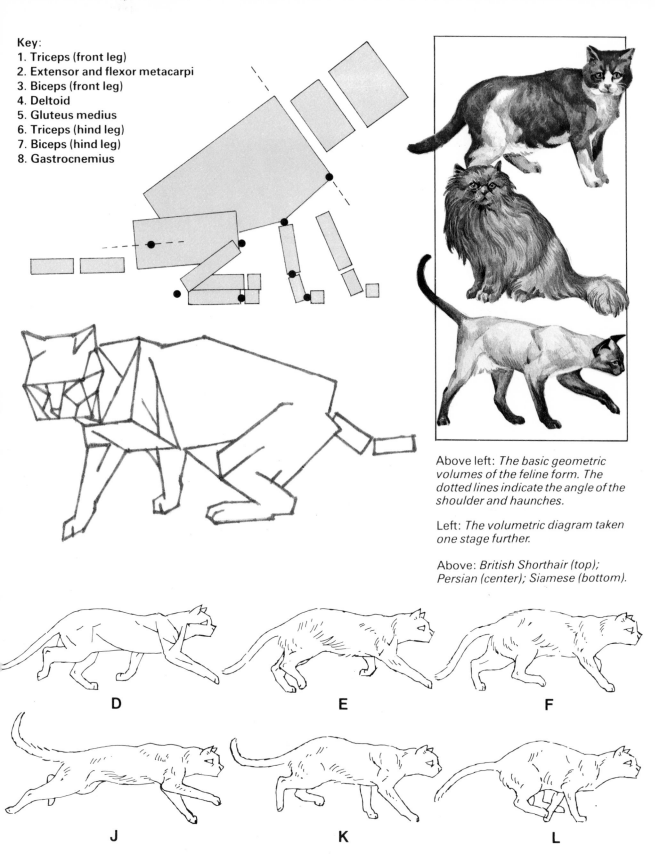

Key:
1. Triceps (front leg)
2. Extensor and flexor metacarpi
3. Biceps (front leg)
4. Deltoid
5. Gluteus medius
6. Triceps (hind leg)
7. Biceps (hind leg)
8. Gastrocnemius

Above left: *The basic geometric volumes of the feline form. The dotted lines indicate the angle of the shoulder and haunches.*

Left: *The volumetric diagram taken one stage further.*

Above: *British Shorthair (top); Persian (center); Siamese (bottom).*

D **E** **F**

J **K** **L**

D. Modify the drawing softening and rounding the shapes to create a more life-like drawing.

E. Finally, indicate the direction of the growth of the fur.

F. This drawing and those on the bottom line (G-L) show the sequence of movement as the walk accelerates to a run.

27

Cats: detail and tackling a subject

Black and white conté crayon on tinted paper was used for this study of a cat because, when smudged, it will suggest the softness of the fur. Pastel or chalk and charcoal can be used instead. Tonal drawing is good experience for working in paint; in both media you have to work in areas, and this involves a different way of thinking. The tones can be blended with a paper stub or with your finger, but do let the color and tone of the paper show through in some areas of the drawing. Use the following procedure:

1. With the corner of a white

Above: *Stages in drawing a cat's head, using conté. The method is described in the text.*

Below: *Apply black and white conté to the area required using a "scribbling" motion. The two colors are then blended with a finger.*

conté crayon, draw the basic construction of the head, marking the positions of the ears, eyes, nose and mouth.

2. Lightly shade in the light areas on the face and background, again using white. Using black conté, lay in the details of the markings and features. Also darken the body – particularly under the chin.

3. Work black and white together to produce gray tones, but retain areas of the paper to keep the drawing vital and lively.

No two individual cats of the same breed have identical markings; even the pattern of each side of one individual can vary. There are, however, certain arrangements of blotches, stripes and spots that are shared in certain breeds. The standard tabby pattern has three dark stripes running down the spine, a butterfly pattern across the shoulders and an "oyster" shaped whorl on the flanks. The legs and tail are ringed. The typical face of the tabby is shown opposite. It has a clearly defined pair of "spectacles" around the eyes and on the forehead a mark like the letter "M". The mackerel form of the tabby type has stripes that run around the body, legs and tail, which is probably the reason for the tabby's other name of "tiger cat".

The drawings of the tabby and Siamese heads show the difference in shape between the basic classifications of short-haired cats, the British short-hair and the Foreign short-hair. The other basic group is the long-haired cat or Persian.

The claws of a cat are normally hidden in an opening at the end of the toe so they remain

2

3

sharp until needed. There are five claws on each front paw: one claw is placed higher up on the inside of the leg (the dew claw). Four claws are present on the back paws.

left front paw

left hind paw

Left: One basic difference between the cat varieties is that of proportion. Compare the heads of a British Shorthair (left) with that of a Siamese. You should attempt to get this correct before proceeding further.

Below left: Once the proportion is fixed, attention can be paid to the detail, such as the paws. Remember, it is not possible to paint in every hair, so don't even try. Flowing suggestion is far more desirable than exact, but tight, statement.

right
front paw

right
hind paw

Horses: basic structure

The modern horse has evolved from a small, lightly built forest-living animal. It had four toes on its front feet and three at the back which splayed out to give it support on the uneven and marshy ground. The third toe was stronger and bore most of the weight. As the animal became larger, the bones between the ankles and the toes lengthened and it began to run on the tip of its toes. It was only when this primitive horse moved onto the firm ground and open grasslands that, through the process of evolution, it began to trot and run on only one toe.

Note, on the illustration top right, that a perpendicular line dropped from the withers passes through the elbow and down the back of the front leg. The shoulder blade is set at approximately 30 degrees to this line. A line produced from the back tendon of each leg extends approximately to the point of the ischium.

A detailed side view of the skeleton is shown in the Introduction to anatomy section. Compare this with the view shown below and see where the bones appear close to the surface.

Key:
1. **The front of the skull (nasal bone).**
2. **The point of the shoulder (top end of humerus).**
3. The front of the breast bone (sternum).
4. The front knee (carpus).
5. **The rear fetlock (top of phalanges).**
6. **The point of the elbow (extension of the ulna).**
7. **The hind knee (the patella).**
8. **The point of the hock (the extension of the tarsus).**
9. **The hip joint (joint of femur with pelvis).**
10. **The point of the buttock (back end of the pelvis or point of the ischium).**
11. **The point of the croup (front, top end of the pelvis).**
12. **The angle of the haunch (front bottom end of pelvis) or point of ilium.**
13. **The withers (dorsal or thoracic vertebrae).**
14. **Wings of atlas (part of cervical vertebrae).**

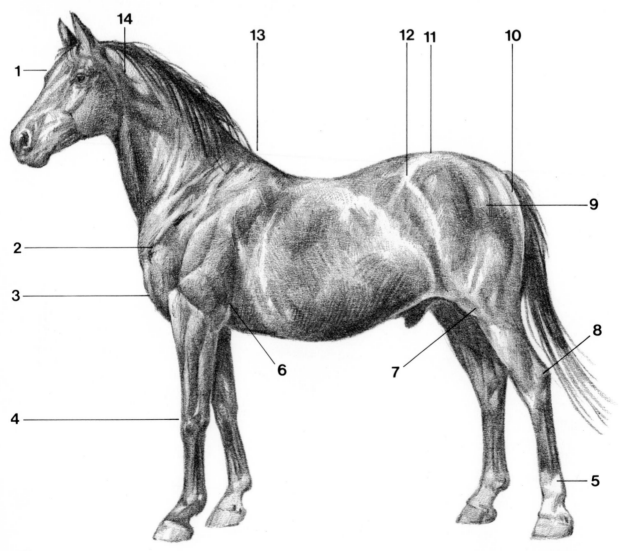

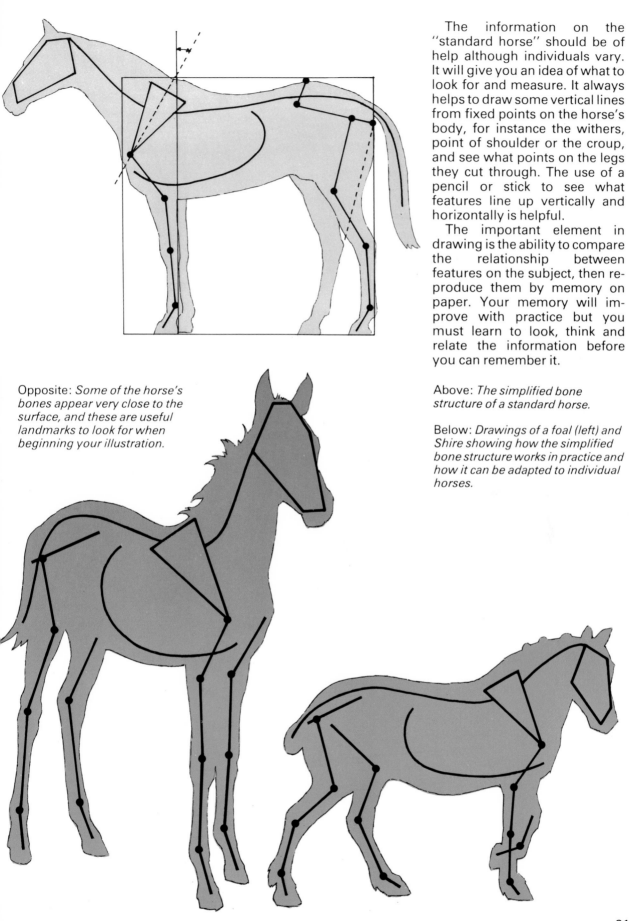

The information on the "standard horse" should be of help although individuals vary. It will give you an idea of what to look for and measure. It always helps to draw some vertical lines from fixed points on the horse's body, for instance the withers, point of shoulder or the croup, and see what points on the legs they cut through. The use of a pencil or stick to see what features line up vertically and horizontally is helpful.

The important element in drawing is the ability to compare the relationship between features on the subject, then reproduce them by memory on paper. Your memory will improve with practice but you must learn to look, think and relate the information before you can remember it.

Opposite: *Some of the horse's bones appear very close to the surface, and these are useful landmarks to look for when beginning your illustration.*

Above: *The simplified bone structure of a standard horse.*

Below: *Drawings of a foal (left) and Shire showing how the simplified bone structure works in practice and how it can be adapted to individual horses.*

Horses: basic form

The muscle structure of a horse is easily observed, the most obvious muscles being indicated on the drawing below. It is even more important to make a careful study of anatomy when drawing horses, as incorrect proportion is immediately noticeable.

The muscles used for running and jumping are well developed. The main masses are concentrated at the buttocks and shoulders and these work the legs by a series of tendons running down and across the leg bones.

The calf muscle (gastrocnemius) is much less obvious than that of the dog as it is overlaid by the massive biceps. Notice also the long vastus, a band of muscle overlying the triceps and biceps. On the forelegs, the triceps are always very obvious.

The diagrams show again how the main body masses can be simplified into box-shaped volumes. The dots mark the main joints. The drawing below this demonstrates how the volumes fit into the more naturalistic body shape.

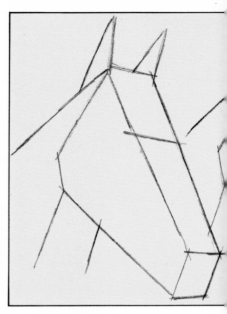

Key:
1. Supra spinatus
2. Deltoid
3. Biceps
4. Extensor metacarpi
5. Extensor pedis
6. Flexor metacarpi
7. Triceps
8. Flexor metatarsi
9. Flexor perforans
10. Gastrocnemius
11. Biceps
12. Long vastus
13. Semitendinosus
14. Gluteus medius

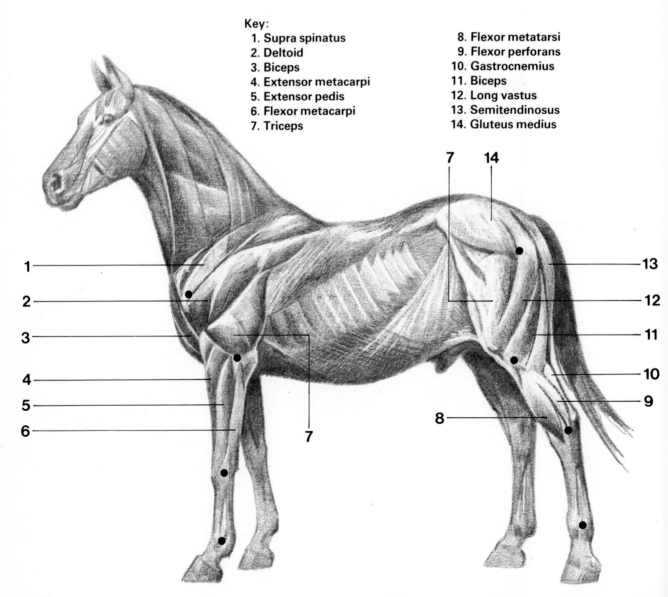

Opposite: *Study of the muscle structure.*

Left: *Stages in drawing a horse's head, progressing from volumetric form to tonal representation.*

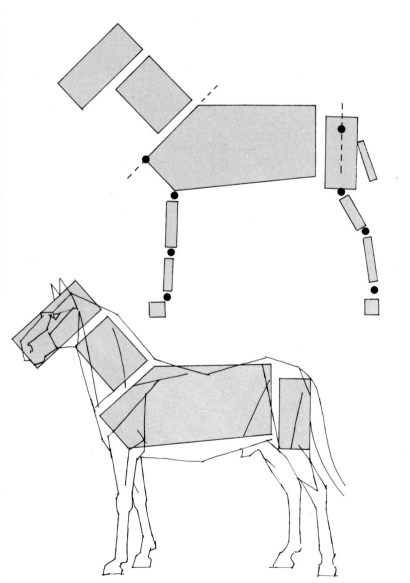

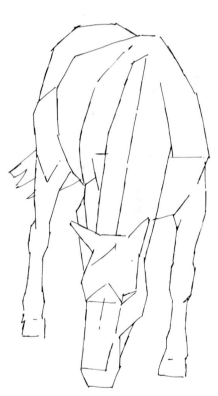

Above center: *Schematic diagram of a horse showing the joints and important angles.*

Left: *Fitting the volumetric form into a more naturalistic body shape.*

Above: *Drawing of a grazing horse shown in the early stages of its development.*

Horses: tackling a subject

There are many different breeds of horse, varying in size from some of the diminutive ponies, like the Shetland, to massive horses like the Shire. While all breeds share a common skeleton (although the Arab has five lumbar vertebrae instead of the usual six), it is surprising how they can vary so much in shape.

Every horse is differently colored or marked. Three examples of color variations are shown, but there are many more. I have also shown some variations in the markings on the face.

The very reflective quality of a shaven dark horse produces

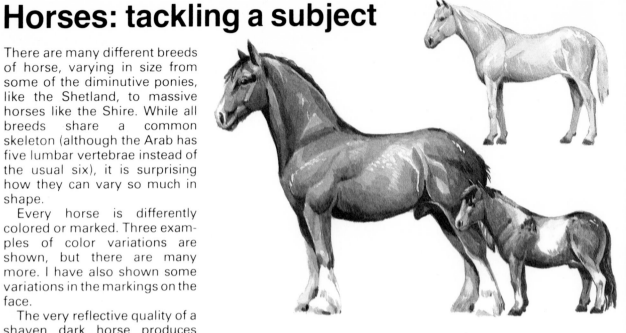

Top and opposite top: *Some of the many different breeds of horse which illustrate individual size and color variations. Markings on the face are particular to each individual horse and can vary from a white blaze to a white star.*

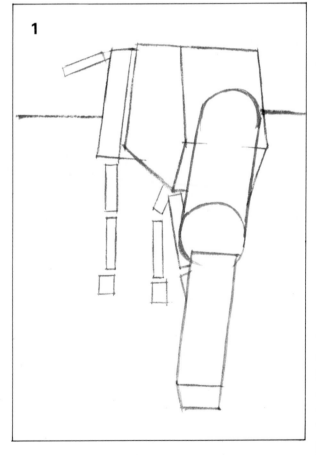

Above: *Mark in the construction of the subject lightly using pencil, charcoal or dilute paint. Adjust the size of the drawing on the paper until you are happy with the composition.*

areas of intense light, particularly on the high spots across the shoulders and haunches and on the flanks where the hair directions conflict. These complications add an interesting challenge to your drawing ability, and mastery of the techniques by which you portray them will increase your drawing skill. To demonstrate the drawing of the horse, black and white paint has been used. It is a good idea to get used to handling paint without the complication of color mixing and harmonizing. A small chisel brush has been used rather than a pointed one to demonstrate a broad treatment capturing the form of the subject rather than its details.

Above: *Block in the background and general shape of the body with mid gray. Try to use the brush in the direction of the slope of the form. Increase the range of grays working up smaller areas.*

Above: *Paint in the white highlights and darken the shadows. Add some detail but do not go too far, nothing makes a painting less life-like than weighing it down with too much closely observed detail.*

Birds: basic form and structure

Although this book is primarily about drawing mammals, many of the larger, more placid birds such as ducks make ideal subjects. You will notice that the skeleton has basic similarities and the bones have the same names.

The shape of a bird is far easier to simplify into geometric shapes – three ovals or ellipses will be enough to suggest the form of most birds. The drawings below illustrate how this is enlarged upon.

In the final drawing, the main feather groups have been indi-cated. The way the wing feathers overlap when the wing is extended or folded should also be noted. All species have a similar number of wing feathers, although the feathers vary in shape to create the most efficient wing shape for the life style.

Below: *The form of many birds can be suggested by using simple geometric shapes. These are then elaborated upon to give a more defined outline. This can then be worked up using color. The illustration top left shows the simplified skeleton superimposed over the basic outline.*

Key:
1. Wing coverts
2. Secondaries
3. Primaries
4. Radius
5. Sternum
6. Tibia/fibula
7. Phalanges
8. Metatarsus
9. Femur
10. Scapula
11. Humerus
12. Ulna
13. Index finger
14. Metacarpus

36

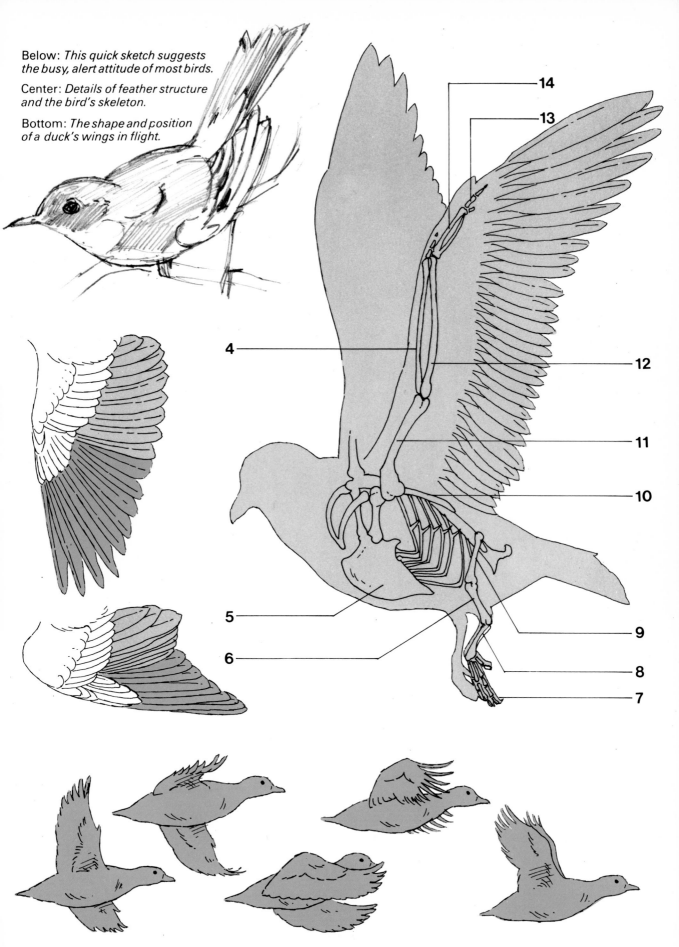

Below: *This quick sketch suggests the busy, alert attitude of most birds.*

Center: *Details of feather structure and the bird's skeleton.*

Bottom: *The shape and position of a duck's wings in flight.*

14

13

4

12

11

10

5

9

6

8

7

Capturing movement

Walking and running animals are, obviously, very difficult to study without the help of photographs. Even the great animal painters like George Stubbs painted a running horse incorrectly, with all four legs outstretched. The development of photography in the nineteenth century revolutionized the way in which artists portrayed animals in motion.

It was Eadweard Muybridge who, by means of action photography, was able to prove that, during a gallop, a horse draws its feet together, and at one point all four feet leave the ground. His work had a great influence on the cowboy paintings of the American artists Remington and Russell and the horse portraits of Sir Alfred Munnings.

A straight photographic copy, however, is rarely satisfactory as it often captures the move-

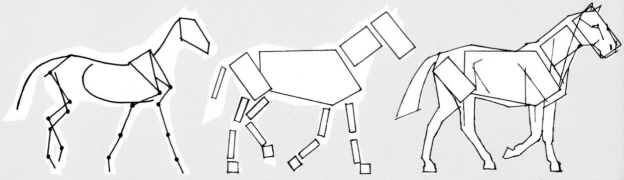

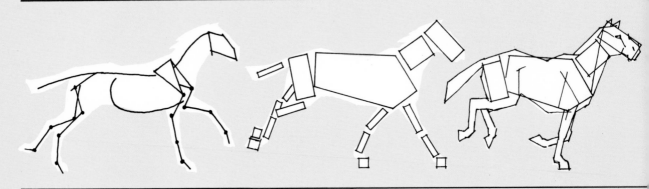

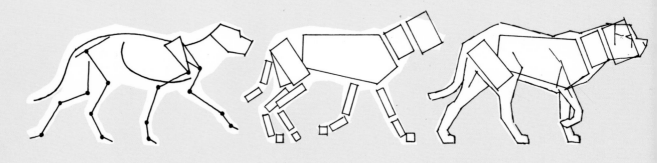

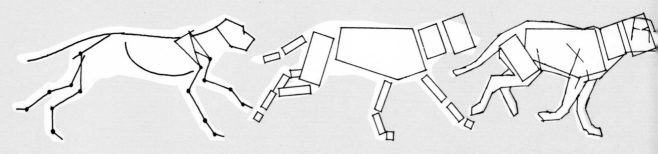

ment at an artistically awkward moment. The feeling of movement of action is best illustrated by portraying the animal in an unbalanced position, for example, with one or more feet off the ground. Try drawing the feet with a little less definition or in a looser manner.

The illustrations below show the drawing methods suggested in this book superimposed on a sequence of photographs by Eadweard Muybridge. The horse and dog are shown walking and running, and the construction shows the progression from the initial axial-skeletal lines through the block form and subsequent stages of refinement to the final use of tone to indicate form.

Below: *Illustrations showing the sequence of movement of a horse and dog in both walking and running attitudes. The basic skeleton is drawn in a simplified form and then information added.*

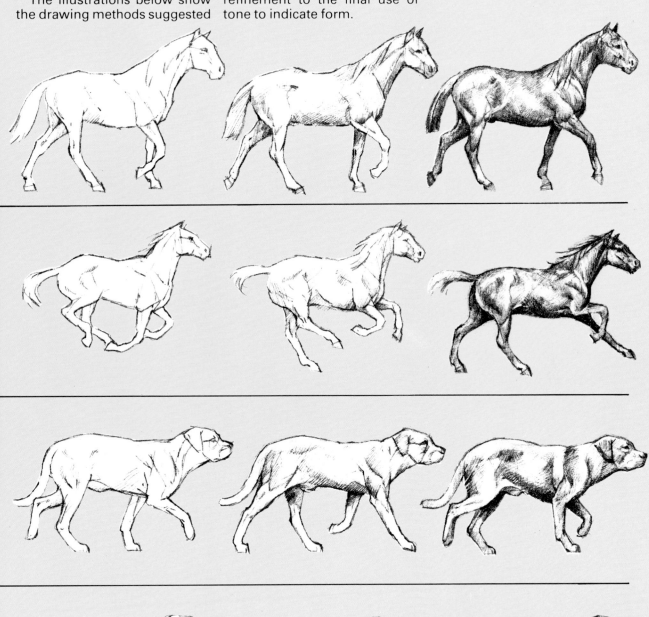

Attitudes

When an animal is not moving, its body or posture can still portray potential movement or action. If you imagine yourself standing, your shoulders may be inclined at a different angle to your hips (haunches). Your weight may be balanced on one leg, and the other leg slightly raised. Your body could be twisted from the waist and your head turned. Each part of your body will be under a different amount of stress and your muscles may be relaxed or under tension. Try to identify this "dramatic" imbalance in your subject. The direction of the spine is the first thing to establish – and is shown by a solid line in the drawings on this page – followed by the angle across the shoulders and haunches (shown by the broken lines). Muscles under stress will be more pronounced, and the skin covering them stretched. The relaxed parts of the body will show folds of fat or skin.

Lines themselves, or the way a drawing is shaded, can create the feeling of life and movement. A line can vary in tension

40

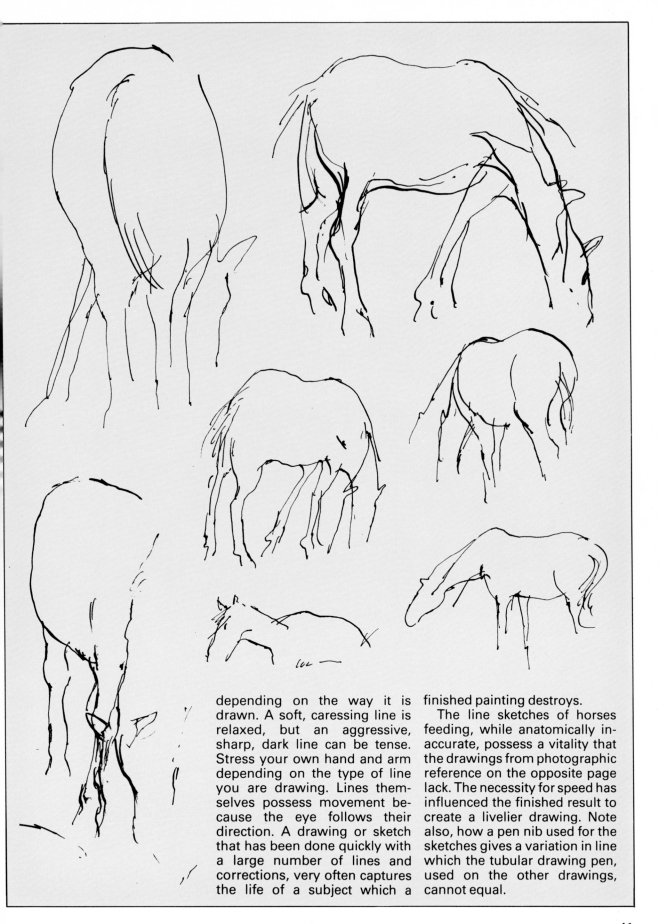

depending on the way it is drawn. A soft, caressing line is relaxed, but an aggressive, sharp, dark line can be tense. Stress your own hand and arm depending on the type of line you are drawing. Lines themselves possess movement because the eye follows their direction. A drawing or sketch that has been done quickly with a large number of lines and corrections, very often captures the life of a subject which a finished painting destroys.

The line sketches of horses feeding, while anatomically inaccurate, possess a vitality that the drawings from photographic reference on the opposite page lack. The necessity for speed has influenced the finished result to create a livelier drawing. Note also, how a pen nib used for the sketches gives a variation in line which the tubular drawing pen, used on the other drawings, cannot equal.

Using color

Color can enrich your work, but it also poses a few problems. Placing colors together and making them work needs experience and sensitivity. It is not just a matter of coloring-in a drawing.

I have already mentioned in the section on materials some of the media that can be used. You can actually draw in color using colored pencils, but to create a wider range of colors there are some that can be blended with water.

Pastels, although they are quick to use, can produce some messy results unless you are experienced. Colors have to be mixed on the paper and cannot be corrected easily. Watercolor in tubes, or gouache, is ideal for learning about color. You have to think about and mix a color before you reach the paper, and this produces a more decisive and clearer mark. You must have a good mixing palette which is cleaned after each piece of work is finished. A porcelain palette with lots of wells is best for watercolor, and a flat board which can be scraped is best for oil or acrylic paint.

Colors work against each other to create space, and that means they can be used to create the illusion of form. The two circular colored areas on page 43 should illustrate this point. The one with "cool" colors like purple, blue and green, in the middle should look concave. The one on the right with the "warmer" colors like the red and orange in the middle should look convex. Color reaction also depends on the amount of each color used or which colors are adjacent, so it is not as simple as these circles suggest.

I have tried to apply this principle to an actual animal. The color reaction between the "cool" and "warm" colors should create the form, without the need for light and dark colors (see top dog's head). In the painting at the bottom of page 43, I have used the natural (local) colors of the dog, but have added tints of the "warm" and "cool" colors. Lighting is the most convincing way to create form. But try to avoid adding black to a color just to make it darker. Add one of the "cool" colors like blue, if you want to

throw the area back or a "warmer" color like purple or brown if it is nearer.

Theoretically, it is possible to mix all colors from combinations of the three primaries — red, yellow and blue. However, there are many colors which are difficult to mix without creating a muddy result. This is particularly true of the purples and browns. There are also many different types of reds, yellows and blues, and only experience will teach you how to mix and harmonize color effectively.

Opposite: *A color circle showing primary and secondary colors using watercolor, oil paint and oil pastel.*

Above: *Two circular colored areas illustrating the way colors tend to come forward (right) or recede according to whether they are "warm" or "cool" colors.*

Left: *The top dog's head, using bright colors, illustrates well the points mentioned above. The bottom dog's head uses "local" colors with "warm" and "cool" colors mixed in to model the form.*

Color and light

Most people will have noticed that a landscape appears to change in color as the lighting changes throughout the day. Monet studied this effect in his famous series of canvases of the front of Rouen Cathedral.

The natural or "local" color of an animal will also appear to change according to the lighting conditions. Look at the changing color of a dog sleeping in the garden as the sun sets.

The Impressionists painted the color of natural objects in many dabs of different colors, which when looked at from a distance recombine in our minds to create the natural color. This is in fact how we physically see color. By subtly altering the size and color of these dabs the Impressionists could capture the effect of light passing over their subject.

I hope my remarks will make you appreciate that there is more to capturing light than just adding white or black to your color. Try to think in terms of changing the hue of a color rather than its tonal value. The insets show a magnified section of the oil painting to demonstrate how a color is built up of brush or pastel marks of differ-

ent colors. If these colors were physically mixed or smudged together they would create a dull gray. The paint or pastel marks can be free and interesting as well as giving the color a richness and an ability to change subtly over a small area. Look at how Bonnard achieved a tremendous richness of color by overlapping brush marks of different colors, or how Degas gave life to his pastel drawings by using different colors.

Left: These two small areas have been filled using oil pastel on the left, and oil paint on the right. It is not necessary to blend your colors to create an illusion of form, in fact it will be more interesting if you don't.

The four illustrations of a dog's head on these pages show the same subject rendered in four different media.
Opposite above: *Oil pastel.*
Opposite below: *Colored pencil.*
Below: *Oil paint.*
Bottom: *Watercolor.*

Watercolor

The beauty of watercolor is its fresh and rather accidental quality achieved by using very liquid paint on wet paper. The transparent nature of the paint allows light to reflect off the white paper underneath giving the colors a luminosity lacking with an opaque paint like gouache or poster paint. Watercolor can be used in a very loose way with a large sable brush, or added to a detailed pencil drawing with a small brush. Because it is transparent the drawing will show through the paint. The traditional approach to applying color is to darken the colors gradually by overlapping washes. Darks are added last and black is avoided, as it tends

to "kill" the very sensitive and subtle color washes. Use a purple mixed with sepia instead, or a "neutral tint," which is a dark blue gray. White produces an opaque paint when mixed with watercolor. Turner used it frequently in a very fluid way and it can be very effective on tinted paper.

In order to use watercolor to the best advantage, application of washes needs to be confident and direct. You must mix your colors on a good mixing palette with wells. Paint in tubes is recommended because you have to physically mix colors. Pans are really only suitable for tinting and sketching. A transparent color will obviously be affected by a color underneath, and you should anticipate this. Too many alterations produce

muddy colors and overworked brush marks. There are many watercolor papers with different textures, degrees of roughness and thickness (weight). It is very much a personal choice, but a smoother finish is better for more detailed work (for this, use hot pressed paper). Your paper will have to be stretched, that is soaked in water, taped down to a board and allowed to dry slowly. As it dries it will contract and produce a flat surface, which will not warp when the wet paint is applied. However, watercolor board, which is more expensive, can save time.

The painting of the dog demonstrates the technique of dampening the area you want to

The illustrations on these pages show some of the different methods and qualities of watercolor.

Below: *The painting of the horse reveals the transparent nature of the paint.*

Opposite above: *The cat's head illustrates the technique of allowing the washes to run together.*

Opposite below: *Dampening the area produces a soft effect without too many brush strokes.*

paint then adding color. This produces a very soft effect without too many brush strokes. The way the colors run together or separate can be very attractive. You must judge when an area is dry before adding sharper details. Paint only the essential marks with as much confidence and speed as you can. Do not spoil the spontaneous quality by adding too much detail.

Right: *Stages in applying washes. Remember, that unless the washes are required to run together each wash must be allowed to dry before the next is added.*

Oil painting

Oil paint offers a richness and depth of color that watercolor does not possess. This richness is increased by the use of linseed oil for mixing. Drying is slow, but there are certain additives and gels which can be mixed with the paint to speed up the process. It is an opaque medium so your drawing is quickly covered and you have to establish and create your form by accurate brush work. However, oil paint, because it is thick, allows the brush marks to be interesting in themselves.

Try to avoid making color changes to the work itself. Use your mixing palette to mix the exact color you want then apply it clearly and with vigour. If the color then appears to be in-correct in relation to the other colors or the original subject, mix a new color and apply this over the first. Never attempt, for example, to make a reddish brown more yellow by the application to the canvas of paint straight from the tube. Even if the color appears correct, the work involved in mixing the paint on the canvas will destroy the life inherent in the brushstrokes.

It is even more important than in watercolor to use color itself to hold the composition of the painting together. Try to see your painting as an abstract as well as an illusion of a three dimensional subject. Turning it upside down or looking at it in a mirror may help.

Use a "sized" canvas or the smooth side of hardboard prepared with white primer. Paint on the primer with a hard brush as this will make a texture that feels good to work on and it will hold the paint. Paint out the white in a neutral color (warm gray) as soon as possible. Unlike watercolor, where you paint from light to dark, white and light colors should be added to the darker tones.

As you proceed with your oil painting and the paint becomes thicker, it is necessary to add extra oil to the pigment. The dictum, "fat on lean" should always be kept in mind. It is a simple process, but essential because the underpainting is usually thinned with spirits, and this evaporates quickly. The dry paint will draw oil from subsequent layers and, unless extra oil has been included to allow for this, the top layer will crack and peel over a period of time.

The illustrations on these pages show a healthy oil painting technique. The brushstrokes are not labored, and lend life to the subject. Some of the initial painting is left to show through while other areas are more thickly covered. The darkest colors are the thinnest so that the canvas is allowed to glow warmly through the pigment. Close inspection of the illustrations will reveal that the warmer whites are in fact the raw canvas which has been left to play its part in the completed painting. This serves to intensify the colors and integrate them into an harmonious whole. Note also the edges of each subject. While some parts of the outline are crisply executed, others are left blurred and this helps to reinforce the solidity of the subject as the planes turn around the form.

Composing your picture

Skill in composition is acquired by trial and error. There are no definite formulae to be learned. The idea is to balance or harmonize the different elements of line, shape, tone and color, but at the same time make an interesting or dramatic arrangement. Hidden within a composition there are dominant lines and directions of shape which lead your eye in and around the picture. A strong directional force can unbalance a composition unless counteracted by another working in an opposite direction.

In the same way, shapes, tones and colors need balancing

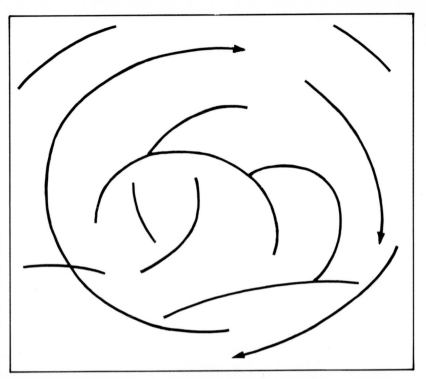

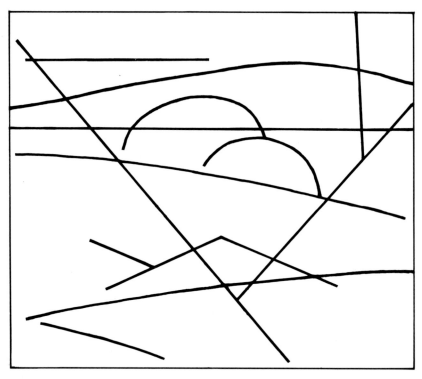

to stop the composition disintegrating or the eye being led out of the picture.

Use the surroundings of your subject to strengthen the composition. The subject should not look as if it has been cut out and stuck on afterwards.

I have drawn a simplified breakdown of the design of the two pictures.

The badger painting is based on a circular design. The dim lighting links the badgers to their surroundings, but some drama is added by the feeling that the animals are emerging and coming forward.

In the painting of a group of lions, the subject is well camouflaged and vanishes into its surroundings. The dead tree provides a strong diagonal which cuts across the picture plane and partly frames the subject.

Painting a dog in watercolor

I have already referred to the use of white in watercolor painting. In this sequence of a Shetland sheepdog, I have tried to demonstrate its use on a tinted Ingres paper.

Watercolor loses some of its "luminosity" on a tinted paper in comparison to the effect of a white ground. The accidental quality of watercolor is largely lost and must be replaced by interesting and detailed brush work. The underlying drawing must be interesting and fairly detailed. It is a good idea to make several pencil studies of parts like the nose and ears beforehand, perhaps in colored pencil. The following sequence was carried out.

1. A very detailed drawing of the head is made in conté pencil, including direction of hair and

detail of eyes, nose and mouth.
2. Using a number 3 sable brush, I apply an underlying wash of paint onto the paper. This is because tinted paper is very porous, and the brush marks will remain much sharper if painted on top of another layer of paint. I leave some areas clear to allow the color of the paper to show through for contrast.
3. The head is basically painted section by section with a small brush (0 or 1). The brush must be of good-quality sable, and with an excellent point. The eyes are painted first to give the subject some "inner life" or personality. I still work using light colors first, in traditional watercolor style.
4. I try not to mix white with the other colors as this will "deaden" them. I use it for the light areas of hair and the highlights on the eyes and nose. Finally, I darken the pupils of the eyes or deep shadows with "neutral tint" and apply a light-blue wash background to set the head off.

4

Painting a dog in oil

Dogs, particularly large breeds with a strong bone and muscle structure, are excellent subjects for exploiting fully the expressive qualities of oil painting. I intend to keep the approach fresh and vigorous but with a little more detail on the head.

I have done several previous drawings of the dog asleep, and chose one to suit the composition I have in mind. Information from all the drawings is used, as it is very unlikely that one study can capture all you need.

1. The dog is first drawn on an oil painting board with a 2B pencil, but charcoal or conté can be used. I have included some soft shading to get a better feeling of the form. Particular attention is paid to the foreshortening of the body and the bones and muscles in the legs.

2. Once the basic drawing is finished, using a chisel brush, I loosely paint the main masses and shadows around and under the dog with light tints of color. At this stage it is possible to stand back from the painting and imagine what it will look like when finished.

Artists often leave parts of their work in this undeveloped state since it expresses the essentials which may later be confused by too much detail. Constable's oil sketches are often regarded with more affection than his finished paintings. The contrast between undeveloped and detailed areas is interesting, and can focus attention on one part of the painting, for example, the eyes.

3. When the underpainting is dry, it is time to tackle in greater detail the tone and colors of the subject. I am now very much aware of creating volume by using color and light and also by the direction of my brush marks.

The brush mark is like the artist's personal fingerprint. It expresses personality and mood. Look at the loose brush work of Munnings's horse paintings. Open brush work lets traces of the undercolor through which enriches the color and texture of your study.

At this stage the whole painting should hold together. Do not try to detail one area at a time as the feeling for the total composition will be lost. Try to keep all areas on the move at the same time and do not get the colors muddy.

It is sometimes a good idea to leave a painting at this stage until you can be more objective in your judgment — it is surprising how you cannot see something wrong or jarring when you are closely involved. Another idea is to look at your work in a mirror. This gives a completely different viewpoint. You should regularly look at your work from a distance to see if it is working; this is why working on an easel is an advantage. A painting is usually looked at from a few feet away. A good painting should work both at a distance and, because of the beauty of its brush marks and color, from very close range indeed.

In an opaque medium like oil or acrylic, radical changes can still be made which will not be obvious later. Never be afraid to correct, as even the correction

1

2

Opposite below: *The initial drawing for this painting of a dog was carried out in pencil. Charcoal or dilute paint would be equally acceptable. Remember, however, when using charcoal or pencil, that excess material must be removed – with an eraser in the case of pencil, and by flicking with a rag when using charcoal.*

Left: *The main areas of color should be blocked in using the largest brush that is suitable for the area to be covered. Keep the painting loose and ignore all detail at this stage.*

3

Below left: *Increase the definition of the form, and correct the color and tone of the painting. Do not scrub at the paint if the color is wrong but change it by mixing a new color and painting over the top. Never take color straight from the tube, but try to mix it with color already on the canvas.*

Bottom: *The painting is completed by adding texture, detail and highlights. Even at this stage, keep the painting broad and do not try to add too much detail. A broad suggestion is far more interesting than an overworked, intricately painted canvas.*

may give life to the painting.
4. Finer detail is added using a smaller brush. The eyes, nose, ears and feet are defined, and I try to achieve the feeling of hair on the body using a small brush. Some areas are lightened and others darkened. The background is repainted to enhance the body of the dog, particularly behind its back and head. The final details on the head are worked in with a smaller brush.

The problem of when to stop is experienced by every artist. I do not want necessarily a very photographic interpretation as I want to communicate my personal reaction and feelings to the subject.

Painting a cat in watercolor

This is a very loose interpretation of a cat, as I am trying to convey the fluffiness and softness of its fur and form. Watercolor is an ideal medium for this, particularly if the paper or board is slightly dampened, allowing the color to spread without leaving many brush marks. You will have to accept that some paintings will work and others will not, but with practice you will learn to anticipate accidental effects. The Chinese are traditionally adept at this and recognize that what is left out is as important as what is put in.

A medium-rough watercolor paper with a textured surface is used. A large sable brush is best for the large areas and a small, fine one for flicking in hair and whiskers. A mixing palette with deep wells and a large jar of clean water is essential, and blotting paper or a sponge is useful for removing excess color.

1

1. There is no preliminary pencil construction; the cat is drawn directly with the brush, keeping the hand off the paper and the paper flat. Draw out the shape in clear water with your large brush and wait a few moments until it has soaked in. Then, using the same brush loaded with liquid paint, wash in the main body of the cat. The paint should spread to the edge of the damp area. The sponge can be used to control the depth of color. Keep the colors soft and the tones light.

2. When the painting is sufficiently dry, add details of paws and head with watery paint for light and dark areas.

3. Finally, using a fine brush with white or dark paint, draw in enough hair lines to suggest the texture. Do not add too much detail, or emphasize the tabby markings, as this tends to confuse the form and ruin the effect.

2

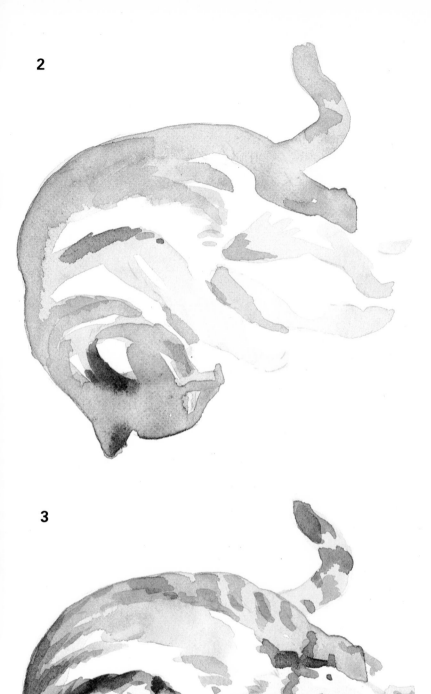

3

This technique needs a lot of practice but it can give some very evocative and pleasing results. It can be used in conjunction with ink drawing where the subject is drawn in waterproof ink, using a flexible nib, brush, or even a stick. When the ink is dry, add watercolor as described above.

When looking at Chinese brush painting in detail, it is surprising to see how much is only suggested detail. The freshness of this kind of work owes much to the ability to capture essential form without running the risk of confusing the eye with excessive detail. I also recommend that you look at the work of the English artist Maurice Wilson, who used this technique to capture the softness of the fur of the cat family.

The art of watercolor painting lies in the ability to control the brush and keep everything clean. While the painting on the opposite page was carried out without use of a pencil, it is not wrong to provide a guide for the eye by sketching lightly in pencil first. Do not use an eraser afterwards. The surface of the paper must be treated gently as it directly controls the quality of the finished result. Never scrub at the paper with the brush.
Color washes should be applied quickly and deftly and then left, otherwise the sparkle will be lost. Finally, keep the first colors applied pale, with plenty of water so that changes, if necessary, can be made using another wash when the first is dry. Changes done in this way will add quality to the finished painting instead of destroying it.

Painting a horse in watercolor

In contrast to the previous method of using watercolor, I intend to use it as an opaque medium by adding white. The effect should be similar to that obtained with gouache. It is a less spontaneous and accidental process involving an accurate pencil construction and careful composition.

I am working on an H.P. (hot-pressed) watercolor board with sable brushes, including a chisel-pointed one. The paint is much less liquid than with the cat study and is applied with short, positive strokes on smaller areas.

The composition of a standing horse from the side is always difficult because it is not a compact shape, and there is a lot of background showing. This composition is rather in the classic style of English eighteenth and nineteenth century horse painters such as Stubbs or Adams, with some background and sky to show the horse off. It will be a formal portrait, being calm rather than dramatic, and the tree, background, clouds and lighting are designed to balance the composition. The head has been raised to make the horse look more alert. Horses usually rest with their heads held down as the photograph shows.

1. Time must be taken over the construction of the horse, and I have almost built it from the skeleton outwards using some shading to indicate the distribution of muscles. The drawing is lightly tinted with transparent watercolor, using the chisel brush. The underlying drawing is still visible, as I add darker washes to build up the basic form of the subject.

2. I now mix an opaque brown (or use gouache), and begin working on the detailed form of the horse, painting with the chisel brush in the direction of the planes of the form, constantly aware of the lighting from the right. The smaller areas on the face and legs are worked with a finer, pointed brush, still working in areas and planes. Individual features have yet to be added. Some solid color is added to the trees and grass, but again, details will come later. The shadows cast by the horse and tree are now added.

3. The horse's body is over-darkened, then toned down by painting over with light colors mixed with white. The highlights and reflections from the skin of the animal are added,

1

2

and the ligaments and bones of the legs defined. The face is worked up in greater detail together with the mane and tail. More detail is added to the background, but it should be left understated to "show-off" the horse itself.

Look at the picture from a distance before deciding which details or areas need lightening or darkening to strengthen the composition.

Opposite below: *The initial drawing will not show under the heavier application of paint.*

Left: *Proceed using the techniques for normal watercolor painting.*

Below: *The painting is worked up using slightly thicker paint. Take care to prevent the colors becoming muddy. Apply highlights deftly.*

3

Painting a bird in watercolor

Large birds with a "solid" form like the pelican are much easier to paint from life than small, nervous birds. Both colored crayon and watercolor – including white – have been used on a light tinted paper.

1. The bird is constructed using the method recommended on pages 36 and 37. Lines indicate the position of the bill and legs.

2. Using colored pencil, add to this basic frame the main shapes of the bill, legs and wings.

3. Some shading is added behind the bird and on its body to suggest its form. More detail is then drawn on the bill and feet.

4. Watercolor is now used to consolidate the solidity and to bring out the shape of the chest and belly.

5. White is used for the first time, to emphasize the form and to make it stand out from the background. The color of the paper is still allowed to show through on the body.

6. Finally, details of the face, bill and legs are added and the drawing generally made crisper by using a fine brush and sharp crayon or pencil.

This is an ideal combination of media for sketching from life in color. Do as much drawing as you can with crayon, adding washes of color if you have time. The late C. F. Tunnicliffe used this technique on tinted paper for his bird sketches.

Painting and drawing birds can be a separate subject in itself. In fact, whatever you find that you prefer to paint will make a suitable point from which to start, because this is exactly what it is – a start. In the end, it is not what you paint that matters, but the work you put into it over the years to increase your experience and expertise.

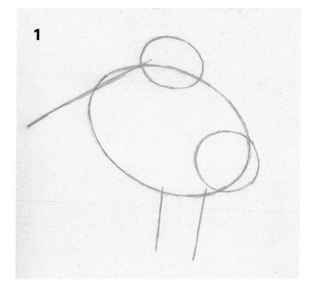

Sketching at the zoo

Because of the generally nervous nature of the animals, much of your drawing from life will remain unfinished, but as you gain confidence you will be able to work with greater speed.

It is a good idea to work on several drawings at the same time, choosing different poses that the subject adopts quite frequently. You will certainly use a lot of paper, but the experience gained in each unfinished sketch will be locked into your memory and will contribute to the standard of your next one. After several drawings, you will be using your growing knowledge of the subject to assist your eyes, and it is difficult to gain this visual experience by drawing from photographs.

The drawings on this page are taken from my own sketchbook. Not every drawing will work well, for time is so vital that there is no time for erasing or making detailed corrections. It can be useful to avoid corrections, perhaps working directly in ink with bold, swift strokes. I prefer to use a drawing pen with a fine

Opposite and below: *Pen and ink drawings of zoo animals taken from the author's sketchbook.*

moulded to a point, and used as a drawing implement.

Do not overburden yourself with materials that you might not need as you may have to pursue your subject at a moment's notice. Your sketch book should have hard covers which act as a support when you are drawing in a standing position but, if you know that your subject will be fairly placid, a larger sheet of paper on a drawing board and a lightweight sketching stool is ideal.

nib and a large capacity of ink, but fine-pointed fountain pens or nylon-tipped pens are also excellent for sketching.

For pencil work I use a mechanical pencil which gives a constant thickness of line and needs no sharpening. Charcoal and conté are also very good for working on large areas of tone, and can be used in holders. Areas of smudged charcoal can be drawn into using a putty or kneaded eraser which can be

Appreciation

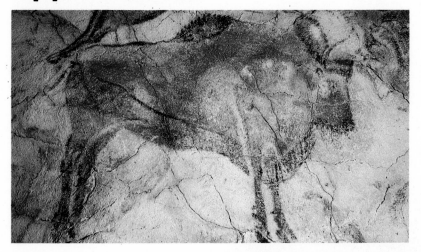

Nothing in art is ever created in a total void, and it is necessary to relate your own attempts to those of other artists, because all animal painters share the same universal problems. By looking at, and analyzing, the way other artists have approached and solved the problems of composition and the description of form and texture, you will be able to draw both help and inspiration from the efforts of those who have preceded you. It must be remembered that what may have been new and inspirational to the artists of earlier periods of art history may appear obvious or perhaps even false to us today.

The English artist George Stubbs, one of whose paintings is reproduced (below), was a man dedicated to accuracy, vision, and non-sentimentality. To the modern eye, however, this work may evoke a sense of the romantic, it being the record of a time and attitude which no longer exists.

The same may be said of the American artist Charles Russell who painted the American West (bottom) in its wild, youthful days. Closer to our own time he, like Stubbs, drew his subject matter from scenes that were familiar to him. In his case, the

popular imagination has overtaken his work. Modern cinema, television and comic books have built upon and made banal the legacy left by a masterly painter.

Finally, consider the cave painting (top) produced from natural pigments such as soot and colored earths. It was painted over 35,000 years ago and the most amazing thing about it must surely be that it will have had few if any precedents. At this period artists, using materials suggested by the color of the beasts they wished to portray, produced an image based entirely upon knowledge gained from personal experience.